Waltisms

Waltisms

A collection of quotes,
proverbs, euphemisms, and sayings

Walter P. Jurek

Copyright © 2025 by Walter P. Jurek

All rights reserved.

No portion of this book may be reproduced in any form without written permission from the publisher or author, except as permitted by U.S. copyright law.

ISBN: 979-8-9928537-0-4

Preface

Over the years, in the many locations I've lived, I have acquired a collection of quotes, proverbs, euphemisms, and sayings. I've come to be known for sharing them with others.

A few of these are original, most are not. Where possible, I have provided the original source and the context.

I have been asked by many to write them down.

So here they are…

You never get a second chance at a first impression.
~ Will Rogers

You are not a cosmic accident

Everyone brightens up a room; some when they enter, others when they leave.

Many hands make light work of big jobs.

No good deed goes unpunished.

The reward for doing a good job is more work.

Work flows to where it gets done.

Two pieces of sophomoric sagacity:

1. The sooner you get behind, the more time you have to catch up;

2. If you wait until the last minute to do something it only takes a minute to get it done.

Shut up and quit whining you little baby.

Cry me a river, build a bridge, and get over it.

Words have meaning.

Pay attention to the units and it will save your bacon.

One must learn a thing by doing it. For though you think you know you have no certainty until you try.
~ Sophocles (from *Women of Trachis* or *The Trachiniae*)

Read a step, do a step, get a banana.

Everybody dies but not everyone lives.
~ William Wallace (Braveheart)

The difference between genius and stupidity is genius has limits.
~ Albert Einstein

Light is faster than sound. That is why some people appear brilliant until you hear them speak.

Stand for something or else you will fall for anything.

You don't know the future so learn all you can as well as you can.

The more I learn, the more I realize how little I know. But it inspires me to go and learn more.

I used to say, "people who think they know everything are particularly annoying to those of us who do."
Now I think to myself, "people who think they know everything are particularly annoying…"

Rationalize = Rational Lies

Expert;
- an "ex" is a has-been
- and a "spurt" is a drip under pressure

Expertise;
- an "ex" is a has-been,
- a "spurt" is a drip under pressure,
- and a "tease" is an undelivered promise

You don't pay twenty bucks to see the clown juggle one ball.

Never mud-wrestle with a pig. You can't win, you get dirty, and the pig likes it.

The average is not always a good measure. I can put one hand in a blast furnace and another in liquid nitrogen. On the average I feel fine but I've lost both hands.

Statistics are like a bikini. What they reveal is very interesting. What they conceal is crucial.

Oh, sorry, did I just pull the scab off that wound? Apply direct pressure and it will stop bleeding soon.
(usually stated in a classroom setting when referring to previously covered subjects)

Opinions are like armpits. Everybody has a couple, and they stink.

House guests are like fish. After 3 days they begin to stink.

Of all the things I've lost, I miss my mind the most.

My brain is full of useless information.
When I recall it, nobody needs it.
When someone needs it, I can't recall it.
Therefore, it is always useless.

I finally figured out what's wrong with my brain.
On the left side, there is nothing right.
On the right side, there is nothing left.

I refuse to have a battle of wits with an unarmed man.

It is better be silent and thought a fool than to open your mouth and remove all doubt.

I do so love mankind; it's the people I can't stand.
~ Linus (from Peanuts by Charles Shulz)

Flexibility eliminates the need for planning.
The key to flexibility is indecision
Therefore, maintain a rigid state of flexibility

Today is the tomorrow you dreamed about yesterday.

A text without a context is a pretext and a pretext is a lie; a half-truth is whole lie.

They say memory is the second thing to go.
I can't remember the first.
It might be hearing...

Insanity is hereditary; you get it from your kids.

God's middle name is coincidence.

It is a pity youth is wasted on the young.

Old age and treachery will always overcome youth and skill.

Technology is wonderful - when it works.

Even a blind squirrel finds a nut once in a while.

Remember, the mighty oak tree was once a little nut that held its ground.

Luck is when preparation meets opportunity

2 definitions of a consultant:
1. Someone you hire for a large sum of money so that you can go wrong with confidence;

2. Someone you hire for a large sum of money who uses your watch to tell you what time it is.

You can pick your friends, and you can pick your nose but you can't pick your friend's nose - unless he is a REALLY good friend.

If your nose runs and your feet smell, you are upside-down.

The answer is only no unless you ask…

I hate it when my fingers forget how to spell.

I'm going crazy and it is a short trip

And this version from my daughter:

Never let anyone drive you crazy.
It's a short trip and you need the exercise.

I am a card, and I need to be dealt with.

The difference between in-laws and outlaws is outlaws are wanted.

Sleeping in the garage does not make one an automobile any more than going to church makes one a Christian.

High five to the forehead
(usually performed immediately upon realizing something that is obvious but has somehow eluded you up until this point)

An elephant is a mouse built to government specs!
~ Steve Mathis (my mentor and friend at my first job out of college)

(fill in the blank) is like calamari, the longer you chew on it, the bigger it gets.
(referring to any subject that appears simple and shallow, but in reality, is much deeper and complex)

You don't have to pay me to be good; I'm good for nothing.

I'm so well-rounded I'm pointless.

There comes a point when you have to shoot the engineers and start production.
~ Steve Mathis

Beauty is only skin deep - ugly goes clear to the bone.

The nice thing about beating your head against a brick wall is it feels so good when you stop.

Of all the days I've had. This is one of them.

Everyone puts their left shoe on last. After you put one on, the other is left.

Caution! Dates on calendar are closer than they appear.

When your mother calls you ought to go.
But when nature calls you've got to go.

Don't practice until you get it right.
Practice until you can't get it wrong.

I'd rather have a bottle in front of me than a frontal lobotomy

The hurrieder I go, the behinder I get.

I'm driving around in circles honking at my own taillights.

I have a great memory.
It's just short.

Reality is for people who can't handle drugs.

When all is said and done; more is said than done.

I'm sorry... did the middle of my sentence interrupt the beginning of yours…

God gave us two ears and one mouth, that must mean listening is twice as important as speaking.

God gave us mouths that close and ears that don't… that should tell us something.
~ Eugene Gladstone O'Neill

Love people, Use things
Lead people, Manage things

Are you dain bramaged?

It's easier to steer a moving truck.

Time flies like an arrow but fruit flies like a banana.
~ Rick Rutledge

Two wrongs don't make a right but two Wrights make an airplane and three rights make a left.

Parents spell love:
O-B-E-Y

Children spell love:
T-I-M-E

90% of the time things will go worse than planned.
The other 10% of the time you have no right to expect that much.

Just because you CAN do a thing doesn't mean you SHOULD do a thing

The epistles were the wives of the apostles.

Yesterday is history, tomorrow is a mystery, today is a gift of God, which is why we call it the present.
~ Bill Keane (quoted in Kung Fu Panda)

When asked,
"What do you do?"

I am an awesome doorstop; I convert oxygen into CO_2 for the plants; and I'll be worm-food when I die!

Despite billions of dollars spent on research each year - death is the number one killer.

When asked,
"Where are you from?"

My mom.

If "pro" is the opposite of "con", then what is the opposite of progress?

When asked,
"How may I help you?"

I'm looking for a sense of purpose in a meaningless world.

Edify, stupid!

I wrote this when I discovered my first grey hair…

Ode to a Grey Hair

> Sparkle, sparkle little hair
> How I wish you were not there
> Atop my forehead you sit so bold
> Telling all I'm getting old
> Yes, you're a token of sagacity
> But I don't care for your tenacity
> What to do I do not know
> Should you stay or should you go
> Dorkel, dorkel little brain
> Thou art shallow and quite vain
> To think a tiny silver hair
> Should be a matter for despair
> I guess with you, I'll be content
> Your color I should not resent
> Having hair is much more fun
> Having grey beats having none

When you muscle your way past the gag reflex, all sorts of food possibilities open up.
~ Ratatouille

Be very careful deciding to what authority you will submit yourself.

Don't look at me in that tone of voice.

True freedom is the ability to decide what authority you will submit to.

Litching sweaters
(a reference to lysdexia, I mean dyslexia).

Don't sweat the petty things; don't pet the sweaty things.

You have to get the em**PHA**sis on the correct syl**LAB**le.

Like a milk bucket under a bull (i.e., useless).

There is a fine line between brilliant and lazy.

Either A, you'll get over it or, B, you won't. I can't think of an option C.

Poor planning on your part does not constitute an emergency on mine.

This doesn't completely suck.
(used as a litotes)

There will be no vacation until morale around here improves.

I've upped my attitude, now up yours!
(learned this one from my Mom)

No matter how others treat you, you are the only one who gets to choose your attitude.

Definition of insanity: doing the same thing over and over expecting different results.
~ Oftentimes attributed to Albert Einstein

Don't go away mad, just go away.

And last, but by no means least, here is the one I think others consider the most popular Waltism:

There is no limit to the amount of straw that can be laden on a camel's back once it has been broken.

~ Steve Mathis

There are more Waltisms, but this gives you the gist (maybe there will be a second book).

Use this page to start your own collection of quotes, proverbs, euphemisms, and sayings

Author Biography

Walt is a quondam Professor of Engineering Mechanics at the USAF Academy, an Instructor of Physics and Engineering at LeTourneau University, a Professor of Science at Grace School of Theology, a veteran home school dad of four now-adult children entering a 2nd generation of home schooling with his grandchildren. Walt is called, designed and equipped to continually learn how God made His universe work and share that knowledge with others so they can know they are not a cosmic accident; they have purpose and value because they are God's workmanship - fearfully and wonderfully made to glorify Him, help others mature, and enjoy a relationship with Him, forever.

www.ingramcontent.com/pod-product-compliance
Lightning Source LLC
Chambersburg PA
CBHW060330050426
42449CB00011B/2718